ROW AFTER ROW

BY JESSICA DICKEY

DRAMATISTS
PLAY SERVICE
INC.

SPECIAL NOTE
Anyone receiving permission to produce ROW AFTER ROW is required to give credit to the Author(s) as sole and exclusive Author(s) of the Play on the title page of all programs distributed in connection with performances of the Play and in all instances in which the title of the Play appears, including printed or digital materials for advertising, publicizing or otherwise exploiting the Play and/or a production thereof. Please see your production license for font size and typeface requirements.

Be advised that there may be additional credits required in all programs and promotional material. Such language will be listed under the "Additional Billing" section of production licenses. It is the licensee's responsibility to ensure any and all required billing is included in the requisite places, per the terms of the license.

SPECIAL NOTE ON SONGS AND RECORDINGS
For performances of copyrighted songs, arrangements or recordings mentioned in these Plays, the permission of the copyright owner(s) must be obtained. Other songs, arrangements or recordings may be substituted provided permission from the copyright owner(s) of such songs, arrangements or recordings is obtained; or songs, arrangements or recordings in the public domain may be substituted.

SPECIAL THANKS

Daniella Topol, Julie Crosby, Kate Pines, Megan Carter, Women's Project, Rosie Benton, P.J. Sosko, Erik Lochtefeld, Clint Ramos, Aaron Meicht, Tyler Micoleau, Toni Press Coffman, Glen Coffman, Winding Road Theater Ensemble, Daniel Talbott and Addie Johnson Talbott and Rising Phoenix and Cino Nights, Mike Kingsbaker, Sevrin Anne Mason, Bjorn Thorstad, Stephan Brackett, Martin and Rochelle Denton and Indie Theater Now, Annie MacRae, David Bradley, Zak Berkman and Abbey Adams and all of the People's Light staff, David Van Asselt, Brian Long, Kate Navin, Kel Haney, Laura Savia and Jenny Gersten from Williamstown, Jody Flader, Jerry Richardson, David Hudson, Lori Wolter Hudson, The New Harmony Project, and last but not least, the Dickey family.

ROW AFTER ROW was presented by Women's Project Theater, (Julie Crosby, Artistic Director; Lisa Fane, Managing Director) at City Center Stage II in New York City, opening on January 23, 2014. It was directed by Daniella Topol; the set and costume designs were by Clint Ramos; the lighting design was by Tyler Micoleau; the sound design was by Broken Chord; the fight choreography was by J. David Brimmer; and the production stage manager was Jess Johnston. The cast was as follows:

LEAH .... Rosie Benton
TOM ....Erik Lochtefeld
CAL ....P.J. Sosko

CHARACTERS

CAL — Mid- to late thirties, bearded, despite often sounding like a d-bag, he is very lovable and likable. Capable of change.

Cal also plays General Longstreet.

TOM — Mid- to late thirties, spectacles, repressed, tries very hard to keep things nice, polite, harmonious. He adores Cal and has fun with him.

Tom also plays the Union Deserter.

LEAH — Mid-thirties, naturally tough and independent, also sensual in an authentic way. She loves a good discussion and holds her own very well.

Leah also plays a Confederate Soldier.

NOTE ABOUT THE TEXT

/ Slashes indicate overlapping
( ) Parenthesis indicate a slight throw away, or slightly lower in volume.

PRODUCTION SUGGESTIONS

The repartee of Cal and Leah should feel a lot like that of Beatrice and Benedick.

In general the pace should be very bright and quick. The speeches can breathe more.

There is a continuity of character between the present day and 1863. Don't feel the need to play them as different people.

I strongly suggest avoiding Southern accents.

The past and the present live very closely together in this play, and figuring out how to express that in the transitions between 1863 and the present is one of the main creative challenges. Having now had the opportunity to participate in three productions of ROW AFTER ROW, I thought it would be helpful to share some of my observations … I'll borrow from two of my collaborators —

Daniella Topol (director for the Women's Project production) often described how the present action would allow the characters to "crack" into the past, like a sudden bolt (with the exception of Longstreet's final speech) … While David Bradley (director for the People's Light production) was fond of saying that journeying back to the present was like passing through a kind of membrane … I like both these descriptions because they are evocative and sensual, but they also allow for mystery. Therefore I suggest: When cracking into the past, be bold, and when slipping back to the present, be sensitive and supple.

—Jessica Dickey
November 2014

ROW AFTER ROW

Longstreet, alone in a single light.

LONGSTREET/CAL. More Perfect … So be it.
(Suddenly lights and sound shift — Pickett's Charge. The sound of a raging battle — marching, bodies, cannon fire, struggle, guns. The roar of war. Watching the charge.) Come on Colonel Pickett swing left
SWING LEFT
Tighten that line boys
Goddamn
DESERTER/TOM. *(Scampers in.)* You did it you piece of shit, you're free! *(The cannons and roar make him cover his ears for a moment.)*
Gotta find shelter
Move your legs and RUN. *(He scampers to another spot.)*
LONGSTREET/CAL. Look at my boys go ATTA BOYS!
Toward the trees!
Goddamn
DESERTER/TOM. Gotta hide 'til the area clears
Gotta hide gotta hide gotta hide gotta hide
LONGSTREET/CAL. My God
There's the stone wall —
My Men! My God!
DESERTER/TOM. There's a house! I see the cellar door — ! *(He runs off.)*
LEAH. *(Clutching a Confederate uniform.)* I've never seen so many men in my life!
They march through town
and I cannot look away!
LONGSTREET/CAL. FIX BAYONETS!
God help us — !
CHARGE!
(A final massive blast. Then — Major lights shift into — The side room

of an old pub in Gettysburg, Pennsylvania. Lots of dark wood, Civil War tchotchkes. Leah is sitting at a small table alone with a beer. She is dressed still in her Civil War re-enactment clothes, a gray uniform. After a moment Tom and Cal enter, deep in fraternal, heated discussion. They are in full, head-to-toe authentic Civil War regalia.)

CAL. Pickett's Charge kills me, dude — it just fuckin' KILLS ME — every year!! The South was WINNING! — until Pickett's Charge!! — And then boom — the tide of the war turned. It could have been prevented.

TOM. That's easy to say cuz it was such a fuckin' disaster. You were very good today, by the way.

CAL. Was I really?

TOM. Oh absolutely dude. You were having a Wargasm.

CAL. *(Genuinely touched.)* Thanks dude. That means a lot. *(Suddenly a school boy.)* Who brought that new cannon?! That thing was THE BOSS. Shouting over that gave me the GIGGLES. *(They stop in their tracks and see Leah sitting at their table. An awkward moment — what to do?)* Um. Ma'am? *(She doesn't look up. Louder.)* Ma'am?

LEAH. Are you talking to me?

TOM. Uh, yeah — Hello — Hi — Have you been — sitting here long?

LEAH. Um — ???

CAL. Did Ron see you come in?

LEAH. Ron?

CAL. Yeah, tall guy, kinda looks like a Sasquatch …

LEAH. Um …

CAL. Yeah, cuz the thing is we usually —

TOM. Yeah, sorry, Hi, what he's trying / — to say —

CAL. Cuz if Ron saw you he probably would've told you —

LEAH. I don't know if it was "Ron" but I mean I ordered my beer … *(Awkward beat.)*

TOM. Okay that's fine, that's cool, UM, we will just sit — um — Somewhere else. That's cool.

CAL. *(Tom.)* (Are you out of your mind?) *(Leah.)* It's just that we usually sit here.

LEAH. Oh. / Uh huh.

TOM. Dude, it's cool, right? No big deal.

CAL. *(Tom.)* No big deal come on buddy this is our night — *(Leah.)* I'm sure you understand — *(He indicates their Civil War re-enactment garb.)* We're kind of traditionalists, if you know what I mean, so …

LEAH. Okay.
TOM. Dude —
CAL. Tom, the lady seems to understand. Am I right?
LEAH. Yeah, I think so. You usually sit here.
CAL. Exactamundo.
TOM. Yes, we do, / but —
CAL. It's a tradition that every year after Gettysburg we come here
and have a beer. Yes.
LEAH. Cool.
CAL. Yes, very. So …
LEAH. So … *(Awkward silence. She gestures to the other seats at the
table.)* You assholes care to join me? *(Not what they were expecting.)*
CAL. That's — not — exactly —
TOM.   — Absolutely. That's very kind of you. *(Tom sits; Cal
complies.)* I'm Tom, 121st Pennsylvania. And this is my comrade Cal.
CAL. General Longstreet. Army of Northern Virginia.
LEAH. Don't mind me. You just do your "annual thing" and I'll
enjoy my beer.
TOM. Oh. Alrighty.
CAL. Suits us just fine. *(They all sit awkwardly and drink their beer.)*
TOM. Well the weather was historically accurate — It was a hot one.
(After a long beat, Tom tries very hard to be congenial, like a host …)
So what were you?
LEAH. Oh we're going to talk?
TOM. Well, sure, why not.
LEAH. Alright then.
TOM. Um — I was just asking, Ms. — ??
LEAH. Leah.
TOM. Leah. What infantry were you?
LEAH. UM — I was Virginia as well. I forget which one. We lost,
I know that. Ha ha.
TOM. Oh, uh huh. Yeah. So you're New. *(With a warning to Cal.)*
Cal, she's New.
LEAH. Yeah. Very New.
TOM. Are you from out of town? Or — ?
LEAH. Yes, out of town. I just moved here actually.
TOM. Oh, I see. That's interesting. Where from?
LEAH. New York.
TOM. New York! New York City? Wowza! You know, I've always
wanted to go to the Second Avenue Deli!

LEAH. It's closed.
TOM. Oh. Well. Welcome to Gettysburg. *(Awkward sipping of beer.)*
CAL. We knew you were New.
TOM. Cal —
LEAH. Oh yeah?
CAL. Yeah, you're Farbing all over the place.
TOM. Oh Christ.
CAL. You're what we call FARBTASTIC.
TOM. Calvin.
LEAH. I don't get it.
TOM. It's nothing. Cal, be a gentleman, okay?
CAL. What? I'm sure the little lady is interested.
TOM. Cal, she's NEW.
CAL. Exactly, so how's she supposed to know?
LEAH. Know what?
CAL. That you're FARBING.
LEAH. What's Farbing?
CAL. What's Farbing she wants to know. Tom, the lady would like
to know what Farbing is.
TOM. Cal. Uh — *(To Leah.)* Farbing is kind of an inside term.
CAL. YEAH
TOM. Among us — re-enactors —
CAL. "Us re-enactors"? Dude, you act like you're ashamed.
TOM. It's when — What? I do not, I am not, I'm not ashamed,
I'm just —
CAL. Okay okay, don't blow your bayonet, I just thought you
sounded ashamed.
TOM. Well, I'm not. I'm not ashamed.
CAL. ("Us re-enactors")
TOM. *(Ignoring him.)* A Farb is when your gear or weaponry or
uniform — uh — isn't up to — uh — ? — par.
LEAH. Par? As in —
TOM. Historical accuracy.
CAL. Yeah, as in WRONG.
LEAH. Huh.
CAL. Yeah, like your nose ring? No. Your jewelry? Uhn uhn. The color
of the wool? Passable. The thread count? No. Mid 1900s, not 1863.
TOM. Okay awesome. Now that we've managed to completely
alienate our new friend here.
LEAH. I still don't understand what Farbing is.

TOM. Farbing is a term used by us — re-enactors
CAL. ("Us re-enactors")
TOM. *(Ignoring him.)* When something in one's uniform or outfit or gear or behavior isn't accurate to the historical context. It's a major concern among us *(Catches himself.)* — UM — among committed re-enactors who — of course — consider themselves Living Historians. If you will.
LEAH. So "Farb" is an acronymn? Or — ?
CAL. No one knows exactly where the term originated. I've Heard Tell —
TOM. (You've heard tell?)
CAL. — that it's a combination of the words "fake" and "garb" — Thusly — "Farb."
TOM. (Thusly?! Wow dude. You're really on a roll here.)
CAL. BUT I PREFER the explanation used by some of the more hard core re-enactors that when we see an improper thread count, or a pair of anachronistic eye-wear, the re-enactor leans in to the Farbing offender and says, "FAR BE IT FROM ME" — to criticize what you're wearing, or whatever … I prefer to think that THAT is where the term "Farb" comes from.
LEAH. "FAR Be it from me."
CAL. Yup.
TOM. "Thusly"
CAL. Farb.
LEAH. Huh.
CAL. You could also just think of it as "Fast And Research-less Buying."
TOM. Anyway. There are some great resources in the local libraries or whatever, or you can even ask other re-enactors in your brigade for help in making sure your gear is appropriate, they can steer you toward the right vendors and such …
CAL. A favorite of mine is Gun Creek Sutlery.
TOM. There's also Rum Creek Sutlers
CAL. Dirty Billy's Hats
TOM. Bug Hill Sutlery
CAL. Patsy's Civil War Buckles
TOM. (that was a great sale last week)
CAL. (Wowza)
TOM. And of course there's our own local Regimental Quartermaster, they're right here in Gettysburg, right on the square there.

CAL. Indeed.

LEAH. So do you guys live in Gettysburg? Am I looking at two typical Gettysburgians?

TOM. Sort of. I've lived here all my life. But I work in Frederick, which is nice, it's got Culture

CAL. Frederick likes to *think* it has Culture

TOM. It does!

CAL. Big fuckin' deal dude you've got a farmers market

TOM. Cal moved here in the sixth grade

CAL. From Virginia. And my first day I sat next to this douchebag in Mr. Putty's Shop Class — (haha! — "Fire it up!" —)

TOM. (Haha — "fire it up!" —)

CAL. And he actually TALKED to me, and like, NOBODY had talked to me all day —

TOM. (Really?)

CAL. Yeah dude — and then that day after school I saw three guys circled around Tom, it looked like there was gonna be some trouble / — and three to one didn't seem right, so I jumped in there. And here we are!

TOM. (They were just jerks)

LEAH. Huh. And so now you re-enact.

TOM. Haha, yeah! I was a big history geek, and I thought Cal would like the Southern angle —

CAL. And so we started doin' road trips every month — Chickamauga, Manassas — we got into it. But lately it's uh — less often.

TOM. (It's still a lot.)

CAL. (No it's not.) *(Quick beat.)*

TOM. Frederick has Good Ol' Boy Sutlery.

CAL. I went in there the other day and saw a decent Confederate jacket for two hundred and fifty.

LEAH. *Dollars?*

CAL. Lasts a lifetime.

TOM. Haha Confederate uniforms are a bit more costly because the jacket is made of jean cloth. Unfortunately there's *reeeeallly* only a handful of people making the proper jean material in the United States today.

LEAH. Uh-huh.

CAL. Your musket is the expense to worry about — that's gonna run ya upwards of six hundred —

LEAH. Are you serious?

CAL. — Plus your dog tent, your canteen, your cup and cooking ware. All Told —

TOM. *(Chuckling.)* ("All Told?" This guy.)

CAL. — it's gonna run ya upwards of fifteen hundred bucks. To get the basics.

LEAH. Jesus.

CAL. Authenticity ain't cheap.

TOM. *(Conciliatory.)* It can seem daunting at first. Most people don't realize the commitment goes beyond sleeping in a tent and wearing wool in July.

LEAH. So you spent fifteen hundred dollars on this stuff?

CAL. Oh no, not US —

LEAH. I was gonna say —

CAL. — I spent fifteen hundred on my weapons alone. My uniform and the extra stuff were another two grand.

TOM. You can imagine that it's not something people do once they start a family (until they're retired or whatever).

CAL. But even if you do get your gear up to historical standards, then there's the fact that you're a woman…

TOM. No, nooooooo, no, that's not a problem.

LEAH. That I'm a woman?

CAL. Yup.

TOM. No it's not. Cal — you know the new rules.

CAL. Oh that is a bunch of mamby pamby bullshit — *(Like a whiny woman.)* "Women can be soldiers too" —

TOM. It was strongly re-affirmed just this year that women can participate in re-enactment combat, / regardless of historical context.

CAL. *(Whiny woman.)* Oh wah wah wah, I wanna be a soldier, / wah wah wah —

TOM. *(Plowing forward.)* And IN FACT — we now know that there were many women who died in the Civil War, serving as spies, nurses, *vivandières*.

CAL. *(Whiny woman.)* I wanna sacrifice History so I feel *EQUAL* — / wah wah wah.

TOM. And of course Dr. Mary Walker won the Medal of Honor for her service in the hospitals

LEAH. Really?

TOM. Yes. Absolutely.

LEAH. Wow — The Medal of Honor.

TOM. It's true. And of course, lest we forget, there WERE actually females who disguised themselves as soldiers in the Civil War.
CAL. (Oh Christ that shit's been beat to goddamn death.)
LEAH. Is that true? There were women who disguised themselves as soldiers? Like passed themselves off as men?
TOM. Absolutely.
CAL. What the fuck is a vivandierey anyway?
TOM. *(Correcting him.)* A *vivandière* is a French term for women who provided soldiers with provisions — food, equipment.
CAL. I know what provisions are, Tom.
TOM. (Alright, I'm just saying.)
CAL. How are we supposed to hold ourselves to historical context if we have skirts running around the battlefield? It's RETARDED.
TOM. *(Loves this.)* RETARDED? Oh now we can say RETARDED? What if there were a retarded person sitting right here, Cal? Huh? What then?
CAL. Oh Christ. You and your freakin' — the school system is making you soft, / my friend —
TOM. No really, Cal, this is important, I want you to picture a little retarded boy sitting right here. Picture him. Picture his eggy eyes and his dropped jaw and lolling tongue and you tell me how it makes him feels to hear you say It's RETARDED.
CAL. I think that's Down's.
TOM. … What?
CAL. I think that's Down's.
TOM. What the fuck are you talking about?
CAL. I think when their eyes are weird and — sort of — bovine — that it's — it's not retarded — it's called Down's.
TOM. Down's? Like Down Syndrome?
CAL. Yeah. Drooling lips. The eyes. That's Down's.
TOM. What is your fucking point?
CAL. That if a little boy of that description were in fact sitting here, he would probably NOT, well, ONE: understand what the fuck we mean when we say RETARDED, and TWO: necessarily be offended because he's not retarded he just has Down's.
TOM. Oh, he "just" has Down's.
CAL. (You know what I'm sayin'.)
LEAH. I think a person with Down's Syndrome is actually considered a person with an Intellectual Disability.
CAL. — An Intellectual Disability??

TOM. Cal. *(A beat.)* Let's move on.
CAL. THE POINT IS — if there WERE a Down's person, who also happened to be retarded, sitting here, we could take it as an opportunity to *confirm* with them that in fact it IS retarded for a woman to be a soldier on the battlefield when there would not have been a woman on the battlefield (in any traditional sense) at Gettysburg in 1863. *(A beat.)*
LEAH. I can kind of see your point on that.
TOM. About the retarded boy?
LEAH. About women on the battlefield.
TOM. Oh, you don't have to —
CAL. THERE, see?!
TOM. No, come on — You don't have to agree with him just because he's fragile.
LEAH. No it's cool.
CAL. I'm not fragile.
LEAH. I get it, I do.
CAL. (Do I seem fragile?)
LEAH. If historical accuracy is really important, it's gotta be a bummer to see a woman on the battlefield.
CAL. YES. Thank you.
LEAH. According to HISTORY, we should be sewing your "freedom flag," or preparing the MEAL over which you discuss your "INALIENABLE RIGHTS."
CAL. Thank / you.
TOM. *(Appreciating her irony.)* That's — huh …
LEAH. I'm sure that IN GENERAL as the rest of the population begins to lobby for equality, if you're part of the group that's always been in power, knowing your time is up must be a BIG FUCKIN' BUZZ KILL. *(Awkward silence.)*
TOM. *(Slight clearing of throat, change of subject.)* So what drew you to Civil War re-enactment?
LEAH. Well, I'm new to the area and I don't really know anyone yet, and I saw an ad at the A&P that the whatever brigade of Virginia was seeking new members for the Gettysburg re-enactment, and I thought Why not.
TOM. But you do have an interest in history …
LEAH. Yeah, I think history is very interesting —
TOM. *(To Cal.)* (See she thinks history is interesting)
LEAH. And when I saw the ad at the A&P I thought well let's just

get right to it — Gettysburg, Pennsylvania — bloodiest battle ever fought on American soil and you could say I have a particular interest in battle — and I didn't feel like playing the SERVING WENCH or a WIDOWED BRIDE or whatever. So here I am.

TOM. Here you are.

CAL. You know if you wanted a battlefield you could've gone over to "cultured" Frederick and done the live action fantasy role-playing group they have. They use potions and foam shields and shit.

LEAH. I don't even know what the fuck you're talking about.

CAL. I'm just saying that just because you're new here and you feel like making friends or whatever doesn't mean you can just show up and ruin what a lot of people —

LEAH. You mean a lot of MEN —

CAL. Have devoted a lot of time and resources to making an authentic acknowledgement of what our ancestors did here. Farbies, man! It's more than just the outfit, I'm tellin' ya!

TOM. Okay, Cal, take it easy, okay?

CAL. Well back me up here, you're sittin' there like a fuckin' TULIP or something, tell her —

TOM. (Look, I'm just sayin' —)

LEAH. You know what fuck you. "This is my battlefield and you gotta play by my little rules" — bullshit / — "Oh wah wah wah I'm a MAN and I'm in CHARGE"

TOM. (oh my god. / Oh god.)

CAL. It IS my / battlefield and the rules are NOT just MINE they belong to HISTORY. /

LEAH. Oh my God —

CAL. This is just your little Saturday entertainment or whatever but REAL *MEN* DIED ON THAT FIELD. *HISTORY.*

LEAH. There was a time when I would've found this interaction with a bona fide MEATHEAD kind of fascinating, but unfortunately you caught me in a DARK YEAR, so I'm going to give you a little EDUCATION —

HISTORY IS JUST THAT.

It's HIS STORY.

And you can roll your eyes and call it a feminist battle cry or whatever but it's the TRUTH.

Just because your team was the only team with a fucking microphone doesn't mean you were the only ones trying to be HEARD. *(Tom starts shredding his napkin.)*

CAL. Oh Christ Tom.
TOM. What I'm sorry
CAL. I hate when you do this dude; it's not —
TOM. Do what? / Do what?
CAL. It's just — It's not —
TOM. I'm not hurting anyone. This is not hurting anyone.
CAL. Stop it. Just stop. Stop.
TOM. You have issues.
CAL. Fuck yes I have issues, we know this.
TOM. Well okay then, I'm not trying to put you down, I'm just defending the expression / of my neurosis.
CAL. You don't see me shredding napkins like a fucking church organist or / something.
TOM. I can't help that this kind of conversation makes me uncomfortable.
CAL. What? Why? We're just having a spirited discussion / here.
TOM. A church organist? Is that what I am if I shred napkins?
CAL. She seems fine.
LEAH. *(Totally sincere.)* I am actually. I've been told by numerous lovers I have issues with aggression. *(Slight pause.)*
CAL. Okay then, there ya go. We're all fine here.
TOM. It's just — The whole men rule the world thing
LEAH. Men DO rule the world.
CAL. Oh come on.
TOM. See, this — this — weird stratification / thing —
LEAH. What? They do.
CAL. Oh okay is that what this awesome feeling is? This nauseous pressure on my chest that I live with every day, no it's not misery, it's just the immeasurable JOY of ruling the world.
LEAH. Well, YOU don't rule the world — / — So that "awesome feeling" is the fact that men DO rule the world and YOU DON'T. You're not a GENERAL, you're MILITIA.
CAL. (Oh thank you for the confirmation.) *(Cal is in her face.)* I play one of the foremost generals of the Confederate Army.
LEAH. *(In his face right back.)* Oh okay
CAL. WHICH IS A PRIVILEGE.
(Leah suddenly kisses Cal on the mouth really hard. Then she sits back and takes a sip of her beer. There is a Big ol' beat of stunned silence.)
TOM. WOWZA   CAL. What Was THAT??
LEAH. I guess I just wanted you to shut your mouth.

CAL. Oh yeah?
LEAH. Yeah. And the other tactics didn't seem to be working, so …
(Cal is completely speechless.)
TOM. *(After a moment.)* Okay.
Let's just — Rest ourselves. Chillax. *(A beat.)*
CAL. (Chillax?)
TOM. (What, my students say it.)
CAL. (Don't say chillax.)
TOM. (My students — okay.) *(Beat.)*
CAL. *(Regrouping; To Leah.)* So how was it today?
LEAH. How was what today?
CAL. Being a man. Did you rule the world?
TOM. Okay okay — let's just — ask in another way, okay?
CAL. What dude I'm just talkin' here —
TOM. I realize you two are practically ENJOYING this incredibly
tense conversation, but some of us don't have the stomach / for so
much —
CAL. We're just talkin' here.
TOM. Well, how about "How was your first re-enactment experience?"
How's that?
CAL. Fine.
TOM. You know what I'm saying?
CAL. No absolutely, you're right.
TOM. Okay. Yeah, just — / you know —
CAL. How was your first re-enactment experience?
TOM. (Thank you.)
CAL. As a MAN
TOM. (Okay —)
CAL. What?
TOM. (Calvin —)
CAL. How was it?
LEAH. It was different than I expected.
CAL. *(To Tom.)* See that wasn't so bad. *(To Leah.)* Please say more.
LEAH. It was definitely interesting …
CAL. This is Pickett's Charge, right?
LEAH. Yeah.
CAL. Okay — Interesting — interesting like …
LEAH. I don't know — Stomping through the fields,
the gear clanging against my thighs and back, making an ugly
bell sound,

my pack against my shoulders …
All the motion of gear on the body,
all these physical sensations were just immediately interesting to me,
like I couldn't stop feeling my body or something,
which actually I haven't been able to do in a long time …
And my legs — my left and my right,
climbing, the swish of grass,
my left and my right,
gliding next to and then past each other …
And even though it's fake, you know? —
you know it's fake —
I still felt scared and excited, a kind of sweaty anticipation.
The sun was high.
There were hundreds of us climbing across this field, toward the trees on the other side, like a wave rising …
And suddenly —
there they were —
the *other* hundreds, wearing the *other* color,
but the same gear, the same pack, the same sweat.
And that's the only clarity there was —
the journey,
the arriving,
seeing them for the first time …
The rest was chaos.
We started charging through the field — and I found myself screaming at the top of my lungs,
just hollering like a fucking lunatic!
How often do you get to do that?! Just ROAR like a fucking WILD BOAR.
And because you WANT to, not because you're in trouble and you have to or whatever …
And yet I kept looking around like, what the fuck are we doing?! Why are we doing this?!
And I kind of loved that — the futility of it, you know?!
And somewhere near the end of the field I decided to get hit and I went down.
Just like that.
And then I just lie there and listened.
To my breath, to the other men charging around me, sometimes over me,

my chest scratched and hot from the charge.
I listened to the earth, the sunshine.
There was a man who went down near me,
and I could see his white hand in the sun,
extra bright, like coral or a flag.
The gentle curl of his fingers in the grass seemed to say,
Touch me;
or —
Let me rest;
or —
Behold;
or —
Soft high five.
(She looks toward the audience.)
And then suddenly I wondered if the dead were watching —
watching us.
Sitting in their invisible chairs, in their invisible rows,
shaking their heads at these crazy assholes who actually want to
relive this terrible moment.
And then I think I took a nap.
The whole thing was more fun — and more sad — than I was expecting.
But after going through it, I can see why people come back.
Keep trying —
To see into that Mirror —
to catch —
a *glimpse* …
(Cal and Tom sit in a thoughtful, brief silence.)
CAL. That was well said.
TOM. It was.
CAL. Some of your Farby points are reduced for stating an authentic
description of the experience.
LEAH. Thank you.
CAL. I'd say that deserves another beer. May I?
LEAH. Um, sure. Thanks.
CAL. Tom? You up for another?
TOM. Sure.
CAL. Alright. *(Cal grabs everyone's glass. Then with a charming little
bow:)* I shall return. *(He goes.)*
TOM. *(Irritated, making light.)* That Guy. *(A beat.)* I saw you today.
I was watching the battle (I was the deserter on the hill there) — I

saw a woman screaming her head off through the charge. Her pony-tail flying behind her. All the men were sort of looking down, but she was somehow — more — UP. Made me want to try it. *(He regards her.)* You're cool.
LEAH. Thanks.
TOM. You are. You're *really* cool.
LEAH. You — seem cool too.
TOM. Oooooh, give it time.
LEAH. So like, what's the deal?
TOM. What's the deal, like am I single?
LEAH. Um, no, that would be a wedding ring on your finger.
TOM. *(Rediscovering his ring.)* Oh — HA HA! — Right. Yes.
LEAH. You — and "That Guy" —
TOM. Yeah — Look — don't — He's not really like this. I mean, HE IS, he is like this, but —
He's just gone through a very bad break-up — like, VERY bad — So he's a little EXTRA —
You're definitely getting the full whammy — the way he just HAMMERS — like … .!!!!
Right? — you know what I'm talking about.
LEAH. I'd say there's some hammerness going on, yes.
TOM. Yes. Thank you. I mean I love him, don't get me wrong — (I mean I don't love him love him — you know what I'm saying) — But sometimes I'm like — why do I hang out with you??!!
LEAH. Why do you?
TOM. (… Yeah.)
LEAH. It's like Lenny and his pet rabbit.
TOM. — Lenny and his pet rabbit?
You mean like — from *Of Mice and Men*?? …
/ (Which one am I?) …
(I'm not his pet rabbit … Am I a pet rabbit?!)
LEAH. Giving me shit for being a woman. Which is kind of IRONIC. A re-enactment for the CIVIL WAR — after which was the Civil Rights Movement, after which was the SUFFRAGE MOVEMENT — and I have to fight for a place at the table? It's like, WHAT YEAR IS IT?
TOM. Hey hey hey! Don't lump me in with him!
I'm my own!
(Leah grabs the gun. Suddenly 1863. Tom is a Union deserter in Leah's cellar. They both hold.)

LEAH. Don't move.
TOM. Please don't turn me in. I know I'm a piece of shit.
LEAH. I said Don't. Move.
Rebs were here this morning, they'll be back.
You can't stay here.
TOM. Please — I just — need a place to rest.
LEAH. Don't we all.
(Beat.) I brought you a clean shirt.
For your gun.
TOM. For my gun? You could've just taken it.
LEAH. There's been enough taking around here. *(She tosses the items at his feet.)* Hand me that uniform behind you. Hurry up. *(He looks around and sees a Confederate jacket and gear.)*
TOM. Why do you have a Confederate uniform in your cellar?
LEAH. Because that's what the dead man on the road was wearing when I dragged his clothes off him. Now: I need to look like a soldier. And you're going to help me.
TOM. What?
LEAH. Look away.
TOM. Why would you want to be a soldier?
LEAH. Look. Away. *(He does. She puts the coat on over her shirt, the haversack, etc.)*
TOM. *(Still facing away.)* I recognize you, you know. I grew up near here. Cashtown. I saw you once, years ago, there was a parade in town and my father took me. You rode the pony. You look the same.
LEAH. Nothing looks the same.
The whole town is upside down — all the trampling, artillery.
All the men have been gone for so long, off fighting —
And then suddenly — behold — more men than I can count.
Their eyes full of blood and smoke, their hair matted,
a smell so sharp it made my tongue move …
And suddenly I had this overwhelming urge —
— To *bite* them — or — *kiss them.*
To put — my — mouth on each and every one of them.
Suck out the anger
and hunger
and homesickness —
and hold it there.
Rip it right out of them and swallow it down.
And that's when I thought —

That's what I'm going to do.
I know it's crazy. I can't explain it.
But I've never been so certain of anything in my entire life.
TOM. You're going — to *kiss* them. *(Tom has turned to look at her and she is dressed as a Confederate.)*
LEAH. That's right. So I need to get into camp. Which means I need to look like a soldier.
TOM. I'm not — good for soldier advice. *(Beat.)*
LEAH. Please.
TOM. Your haversack is wrong.
LEAH. *(Gun back down.)* My what?
TOM. Your haversack. Here, it goes — they wear it on the other … *(He tentatively goes over to her and adjusts her haversack, and then her canteen and gun powder.)*
And your gun powder is on the other side, your right there.
Do you know how to hold the gun? When you're marching you put it on your shoulder, like this. Hook it on your shoulder, like that, then this part can rest on your elbow.
LEAH. It's heavy.
TOM. It should be, considering what it's for.
Now if you have to shoot it —
LEAH. *(Fuck off.)* I know how to shoot it.
TOM. Alright then.
You look good. I mean not "good."
LEAH. *(Don't get fresh.)* (Alright.)
TOM. You look — you'll pass. For a man.
LEAH. Good. *(Tom removes his blue coat and undershirt.)*
TOM. Here, take this. I'll leave it here. When you're done kissing the Confederates, you can start on the Union.
LEAH. But — won't you need it?
TOM. No. I'm not — … No. *(Beat. He puts on the shirt she gave him.)*
LEAH. *(As he puts it on.)* That was my father's.
TOM. It fits.
LEAH. You can stay. Here in the cellar.
TOM. — Thank you. *(A beat between them.)*
LEAH. Good luck, soldier.
TOM. Good luck to you.
Soldier.
(They return to the bar. Beat.)

LEAH. I'm not really, uh, at my best right now. I mean, I put my finger on the map one drunken night about three weeks ago and it landed on Gettysburg, Pennsylvania.
TOM. I'm sorry I think I need my ears cleaned — did you just say *you put your finger on the map one drunken night??!*
LEAH. Yeah.
TOM. What made you do that?
LEAH. Despair.
TOM. Despair.
LEAH. Yeah. Ten years as a modern dancer will do that to you.
TOM. A modern dancer — wowza — you don't meet one of those every day.
LEAH. I'm not sure you're meeting one now. I won't bore you with the slow gasping RETREAT of my dance career — it's a really hard life, once you reach a certain age your viability is sort of gone, blah blah blah ... So I got a job at the Jo-Ann Fabrics on Route 30. College graduate, now making $11.95 an hour. And here I am.
TOM. Wowza.
LEAH. I just — need to be somewhere quiet, where I can just — hunker down, let the smoke clear, assess the damage. Then I'll regroup.
TOM. I'm about to have a son. *(Cal has entered with the beers. He listens, unseen.)*
LEAH. Wow.
TOM. Yeah, it's very… All day I kept thinking, I'm going to be a father.
It's supposed to be fun, we re-enact to have fun, and it's also a kind of patriotism, there are flags everywhere, we sing the National Anthem at the top ... But in light of my son's pending arrival, it wasn't fun. I just kept thinking …
How will I make sure he is treated justly?
How will I insure his tranquility?
How will I provide for his defense, his welfare …
All day I was looking down the barrel of that gun.
(Pun — kind of — intended.) *(Cal steps forward with the beers.)*
CAL. Sorry I took so long — What did I miss? *(Teasing Tom.)* Any KISSING?!!?
LEAH. *(Provocative.)* MAYBE. Maybe you missed a lot of kissing Cal.

TOM. *(Defensive.)* Noooo. No. No.

TOM. (You didn't.)

LEAH. *(Looking to Tom.)* Tom and I were just — discussing the day. *(Beat between Tom and Leah.)*
CAL. *(Some kind of serving wench character.)* A brew for you, *my lady*. A brew for you, Captain Chub.
TOM. Why do you have to do that? / Draw attention to gender like that? It's — it's just not — it's not —
CAL. (Do what? — be a charming son of a gun? Hee hee!)
LEAH. *(Shifting gears.)* So like where are all the black people? *(Beat.)*
TOM. Um — ?   CAL. You mean like, *right now*?
LEAH. No I mean like, all day today I didn't see any black people. Re-enactment for the Civil War and there are no black people??? There were over two hundred thousand people there, maybe MORE, and I counted TWELVE black people. I saw FOUR ASIANS. You get what I'm saying?
TOM. I'm Jewish. Just sayin'.
LEAH. You don't have Jews here either?! / (Jesus where have I moved to?)
CAL. Yeah, growing up around here, Tommy was the Jew Kid. *(Points to himself.)* White Trash. *(Points to Tom.)* Jew Kid. It was a match. *(Sings to Tom.) Where would I beeeee without yoouuuu? How would I evah, evah surviiiivveee?*
TOM. You make a good point — re-enactors are categorically, predominantly, uh, white.
LEAH. And male.
TOM. Indeed.
LEAH. Maybe people who aren't white men don't feel so welcome. Maybe.
CAL. Alright you two — let's not.
LEAH. I don't think there's even a black person in this bar. I saw one guy that MIGHT be Hispanic, but it's also possible he was just tan.
CAL. I think most of the black guys on my crew go to Pappy's, the bar on Route 30. (My construction crew.) I go there every now and then. They've got a dart board.
TOM. There *are* black re-enactors, you know.
LEAH. Really?
TOM. / Indeed.
CAL. Oh yeah. There's Lawrence Daily over in Frederick — / he's the one who hooked me up with the saber salesmen two years ago.
TOM. *(Points for Frederick on the Culture scale.)* (Frederick. Just sayin'.)

CAL. And I think Mike James goes with him sometimes. That guy's got a great truck.

TOM. Most people don't know that about a hundred and eighty thousand African Americans fought in the Civil War. Though awareness is growing — Most people know about the 54th Massachusetts, from the movie *Glory* — ?

LEAH. (Amazing movie)

TOM. (Amazing movie) — So there are black re-enactors to, you know, honor that legacy. And apparently there are even blacks who re-enact for the *Confederacy*, because (apparently) historians now assert that there were blacks who FOUGHT for the Confederacy. And SOMEDAY, if you get me good and drunk, I will REGALE you with the many fine and fascinating details of the JEWS and the Civil War!

CAL. Oh look out! Tommy here can wax REAL poetic on the war prowess of the Jews circa 1863. (Especially if a little Southern Comfort is involved haha.)

LEAH. So you're like a major history buff.

TOM. I'm an American History teacher.

LEAH. No shit.

CAL. Oh, dude — I've been so happy to see you we haven't even talked about the fuckin' STRIKE. *(Big ol' icy beat.)*

TOM. How do you even know about that?

CAL. Frederick may be far enough that we never see each other, but it's not too far to be local news. *(Beat.)*

LEAH. This is a teacher strike?

CAL. Tom's going on strike. Come on, tell me all the details, what's the plan of attack?

TOM. I don't know yet — I really don't wanna talk about it.

CAL. Deadline's coming up, right?

TOM. Well, yeah, it's tonight —

CAL. Tonight??

LEAH. What's tonight?

TOM. *(Removing the contract from his pants pocket.)* Well, it's a long and very complicated story, but basically tonight I have to decide whether or not I'm gonna sign this piece of paper and agree to the budget cuts, or if I'm gonna go on strike with the other teachers.

LEAH. That sucks.   CAL. Um. Whoah whoah whoah.

TOM. What?

CAL. *(Tom's contract.)* What do you mean "what"? Dude.

TOM. Oh Christ.

CAL. You had that on you in the battle?

TOM. Yes Cal, yes, so what. So what?

CAL. (So what? What are you talking about, so what?)

LEAH. Wait, I don't understand

CAL. "Us re-enactors" would not have carried a document from contemporary life, printed on a fuckin' laser printer, during a re-enactment of 1863. Not done.

TOM. Look I know it wasn't cool, but I thought bringing it with me on the field would help me — I don't know — help me decide what to do.

CAL. (Okay fuck the paper) What's to decide? The school district is a bunch of assholes.

TOM. Budget cuts.

CAL. Budget cuts? I'd like to know if the superintendent is taking a budget cut.

LEAH. Exactly. I love how there's still a fuckin' aristocracy in this country.

CAL. WORD.

So you're gonna strike, right?

TOM. It's not that simple. I mean first of all we probably won't win.

CAL. What do you mean? You could win. Especially if the teachers stick together. And so what if you lose? There's something to be said for fighting the fight, even if you might lose. That's the amazing thing about Pickett's Charge, right?

TOM. Cal, come on —

CAL. No I'm serious dude. Pickett's Charge is about courage.

You know the story well —

Both armies had suffered unprecedented casualties the first two days of Gettysburg —

The Union Army, SLAUGHTERED the day before, have held the high ground.

And the Confederates, equally decimated, start here …

TOM. Jesus Christ I know this!

CAL. So get into it. It's all there for you.

TOM. Leah, you don't want to hear anymore Civil War shit, do you?

LEAH. Maybe I do.

CAL. The Confederate long range artillery was supposed to have started first thing, right?

TOM. Yes, to wipe out some of the Union's artillery.

CAL. And for whatever reason …

TOM. Colonel Alexander was delayed.

CAL. That's right. So an already risky battle plan was getting riskier by the minute. But despite Longstreet's warning, they proceed with the charge. The rebels walked into this open field, a mile of marching ahead of them — long range artillery firing away, thousands of men waiting on the ridge to kill them — and they made it all the way across Emmittsburg Road, long range cannon fire, death all around, they could've turned back — they passed Codori farm, around here, now within rifle range, "the air thick with lead" — they could've turned back — they got all the way to the stone wall, where it turned into a fuckin' bloodbath — Bayonets stabbing, guns firing like three feet away, *punching* …

TOM. The courage of that.

How did they do that?

I wish I could just drop myself in front of that wave —

That front row of

Blind,

Devoted

Men,

Put my face in front of theirs,

that WILL —

and MATCH IT.

As if by forming myself to their image, I might know …

CAL. Look if you know what's right, you charge that field! You fucking STRIKE!

TOM. It's not that simple, Cal! There are COSTS, you know!?!? It's not just "right" at all costs. What about your family? What about your own stupid little life? Nothing is that right. Nothing is so right that it doesn't matter what you lose for it.

CAL. Sir you are standing on the very ground where our ancestors did JUST THAT.

(Cal is Longstreet. Tom is the Union deserter, hands bound. 1863.)

LONGSTREET/CAL. *(To the deserter/Tom.)* So what was the plan? Were you just gonna hide in that cellar? *(Leah now dressed as a Confederate steps forward.)*

LEAH. Sir, you requested some assistance. *(She suddenly sees the Union deserter/Tom. They make eye contact.)*

LONGSTREET/CAL. Yes — we found this prisoner when we were scouting for a field hospital. I need someone to guard him.

LEAH. … Yes sir.

LONGSTREET/CAL.   Where is our long range artillery?? It should've started hours ago! I'm not sending my men across that open field under full enemy fire! If Colonel Alexander does not take out some of their long range artillery I swear to God I'm going to have a HUMAN BABY right here on this goddamn spot.

LEAH. *(A human baby?)* Yes sir.

LONGSTREET/CAL.   *(Returning to the deserter.)* Now, where were we? *(But then suddenly notices.)*

Private, adjust your haversack.

LEAH. (Dammit.)

LONGSTREET/CAL. I don't appreciate slovenliness.

LEAH. No sir.

DESERTER/TOM. *(Distracting Longstreet to help Leah.)* — Uh — I didn't want to hide. I just didn't want to fight.

LONGSTREET/CAL. *(Turning back to him.)* Oh? And why is that?

DESERTER/TOM. I can't shoot.

LONGSTREET/CAL. (The Union army is goddamn amazing.) You can't shoot a gun?

DESERTER/TOM. No sir. A person.

LONGSTREET/CAL. A person?

DESERTER/TOM. I can't shoot a person.

LONGSTREET/CAL. … Why not?

DESERTER/TOM. …

LONGSTREET/CAL. Come on. I'm not moving 'til that artillery begins. Why not?

DESERTER/TOM. — What if I'm wrong?

LONGSTREET/CAL. What do you mean?

DESERTER/TOM. What if someday

there they are, sitting up,

Looking right at me …

What if I have to answer to them?

LONGSTREET/CAL. *(Quietly, deeply serious.)* … It's a *WAR.* *(Beat. Longstreet takes off his hat in frustration and shakes the dirt off of it.)* Is it always like this, so goddamn humid? Makes you miss Virginia — the Virginia shade is considerable.

DESERTER/TOM. I've never been.

LONGSTREET/CAL. *You've not been to Virginia??*

DESERTER/TOM. My father's been to Georgia.

LONGSTREET/CAL. And what brought him to Georgia?

DESERTER/TOM. There was a large fire in the town of Gainesville, my father led a group of men went down to rebuild. *(Small beat.)*
LONGSTREET/CAL.   I remember that fire. And your father went down to rebuild? What does your father do?
DESERTER/TOM. He's a rabbi.
LONGSTREET/CAL. A rabbi's son. That musta been hard.
DESERTER/TOM. It's hard to be anyone's son.
LONGSTREET/CAL. Well ain't that the goddamn truth.
I could never go in for all that.
God's love, the Bible. Supposed to be Perfect, aren't they?
And we're supposed to emulate that or something.
But I don't know what Perfect is.
Before this war I'd have had you shot. Or hung.
And here I am having a goddamn CHAT. Nothing makes any goddamn sense.
This morning at breakfast they were discussing a rumor:
Apparently —
Several men in the camp have been visited by a kind of —
Female Spirit — dressed as a soldier, who comes to the men at night.
They wake up, and there's a woman in their tent,
(dressed in a full goddamn uniform mind you) —
She sits next to them, she looks down, and she *kisses them.*
Then she's gone. Like a dream. *(Beat.)*
DESERTER/TOM. *(Maybe stealing a glance over to Leah.)* Sounds nice.
LONGSTREET/CAL. You know what sounds nice?
Pulling all of my men into the crook of my arms
And taking them as far as possible from that goddamn field.
(Longstreet puts his gloved hand over his face. His beard trembles. The Union deserter doesn't know what to do. He tentatively inches over to Longstreet, stands nearer to him. Longstreet doesn't move away.)
DESERTER/TOM. *(After a moment — gently.)*
I think —
it's not about
Perfect. Sir.

…

The idea is not to be
Perfect.
But to be

More
Perfect.
Sir.
LONGSTREET/CAL. *More* Perfect.
DESERTER/TOM. Yes sir.
I think that's nearer the point.
Or at least I hope so.
Sir. *(Colonel Alexander's big guns have started their assault.)*
LONGSTREET/CAL. Sounds like Colonel Alexander has decided
to join our cause.
LEAH. Yes sir.
LONGSTREET/CAL. Very well, let's … *(Longstreet suddenly notices
something is off.)* — What is your name soldier?
LEAH. Me? Private Louis, sir. *(Is the soldier — pretty?)*
LONGSTREET/CAL. *(Slowly.)* Private Louis — you have a
remarkably close shave.
LEAH. *(Making brief eye contact with the Union deserter.)* … Thank
you sir.
LONGSTREET/CAL. *(A decision.)* Private Louis, take this young
man to the cellar where we found him, and leave him there.
DESERTER/TOM. *(Surprised.)* — Sir?
LONGSTREET/CAL. *(To the deserter, with sudden, quiet intensity.)*
You run — away from this battle — you run to your father's house.
DESERTER/TOM. And do what sir?
LONGSTREET/CAL. You tell him … That General Longstreet,
raised in Gainesville,
sends his regards.
Do you understand? *(Deserter/Tom just stares at him.)*
Private Louis — send word to Colonel Pickett and the others that
we begin our charge momentarily.
LEAH. *(Beginning to take Tom away.)* Yes sir. *(Longstreet/Cal stares
at the open field, then takes hold of the deserter/Tom's arm.)*
LONGSTREET/CAL. *(Afraid, the charge upon him.)* More Perfect …
So be it.
(Lights gently return.)
Of course there will be COSTS. If you believe in your Cause, you
accept the costs. / I'm just trying to help you do the right thing here.
TOM. Cal. Enough. Just … Enough.
CAL. If I were you I would strike.

TOM. Duly noted. *(A long awkward beat. They become aware of Leah again.)*
CAL. Oh damn. Sorry Leah. Bunch of douchebags havin’ a Man Session here.
LEAH. That’s okay. *(Another small beat.)*
TOM. Leah was a modern dancer.
CAL. No shit. Like Martha Graham and Merce Cunningham and whatever?
TOM. *Merce Cunningham??*   LEAH. Wow.
What’s Merce Cunningham?
CAL. He did this weird thing where like, the music and the dance were separate.
TOM. What??
CAL. Like the music might be going — *(Sings.) Blah-di-blah-di-blah*
And then the dance might be going —
(He demonstrates something completely different than the music.)
And Martha Graham was like —
(He does some abdominal Martha Graham-ish move.)
You know. Martha Graham.
TOM. *(Bewildered/disturbed.)* Appalling.   LEAH. (Wow.)
CAL. *(To Leah.)* Am I right?
LEAH. Not wrong. / (Not *right*, but …)
TOM. How the hell do you know about Modern Dance?
CAL. *(Duh.)* I watch PBS.
LEAH. Didn’t see that coming, not gonna lie.
CAL. Gettysburg must seem like a bunch of hicks to you.
LEAH. Jury is still out.
CAL. I’m fuckin’ proud to live in Gettysburg.
LEAH. Why? *You* didn’t do anything.
CAL. Sure I did. I do it every year.
LEAH. What, you’re like, honorable by proxy??
CAL. Yeah. We’re like, Sentinels of the Legacy. *(Small beat.)*
LEAH. *Sentinels of the Legacy.*   TOM. You sound like a douchebag.
                              You really do.
CAL. You know what I’m saying. Gettysburg is a special place.
TOM. I love being so near the Mason-Dixon Line. There’s something very beautiful about it.
LEAH. What does it look like — the Mason-Dixon line?
TOM. Well, from the road you can almost miss it — it’s just a small sign that says, you know, “Mason-Dixon Line.” But then

there's usually some kind of natural landmark that delineates it, like a line of trees. *(He uses his hands to show the trees.)*
Sort of like a row of hands.
A row of hands saying, like, "Hold."
LEAH. Whoah.
TOM. It's deep. That line is deep.
CAL. Like that line in that play — "Attention must be paid" — what was that from?
Life of a Salesman?
TOM. Dude, where are you   LEAH. (Death. Death of a.)
getting this shit?
CAL. What?
TOM. The dance stuff, now a line from a play, like who are you?
CAL. If you'd hang out with me more often you'd know. /
Just sayin'.
TOM. What do you think I'm doing now?
CAL. This doesn't count!
TOM. Why not?
CAL. Cuz we do this every year dude. This is required.
Gettysburg is required. Pickett's Charge is required.
TOM. Required? What does that mean?
CAL. You haven't returned my calls you asshole. I've been calling you man. I know you're doing summer school and Carrie is ready to pop, but like, come on. Doing this shit together is one thing, that's bare minimum but what about real life? I need you right now. And I feel like I had to drag you even to do THIS!
TOM. Look Cal — I've got a lot going on right now too you know, the strike, the baby.
I usually love it — the battle, the people —
But today I just kept thinking, I come play soldier at Gettysburg because let's face it —
I'm gonna go home and have dreams and get up and go teach,
and go home and have dreams and get up and go teach,
and have a holiday because it's time to have a holiday,
then go home and have dreams and get up and go teach.
And what the fuck is wrong with that?!?!
I hate this fucking piece of paper!
This piece of paper makes me feel like a piece of shit.
I'm so sick of only having $168 extra a month — for anything — a beer or a birthday —

I don't need to be rich or anything, but $168? It's no fucking life.
It makes me want to just kick something. Or stab it.
Just kick it and stab it and — kick it — and tell it not to fucking
tread on me.
CAL. Dude, it sounds like you want to strike.
TOM. Yes, Cal I want to strike but I also want to sign. Don't control
me, okay? / Ever since we were kids, you've always — just —
CHARGED, you know? But like, some of us aren't like that, okay?
CAL. (Controlling — I'm not controlling you.)
TOM. I just want to do my fucking job — I don't want to have to
DEFEND my whatever —
I could totally shove a bayonet into that cheap-ass superintendent.
LEAH. Fuck that douchebag.
TOM. FUCK
THAT
DOUCHEBAG.
CAL. Yeah buddy that's what I'm talkin' about! Stabbing someone
with a bayonet! Can you imagine actually doing that?
LEAH. Definitely. *(Cal and Tom look at Leah.)*
CAL. You can.
LEAH. *(Dead serious.)* Yeah.
CAL. Really.
LEAH. Yeah.
CAL. A bayonet into another man's *body*…? You could do that…?
LEAH. Yes. I could do that.
CAL. No way.
LEAH. Why do you say that?
CAL. Because that's just not natural. There is nothing natural
about shoving a bayonet into another man's body.
LEAH. When your life is in danger? You'd be surprised.
CAL. Well, sure, thousands of soldiers did it, I'm just saying there's
nothing natural about it. Not like any of us here would actually
know about this because we live in the twenty-first and we don't
really have to fight for our lives on a regular basis or anything.
LEAH. I have fought for my life.
CAL. No, I don't mean like metaphorical, Joseph Campbell kind
of shit —
LEAH. Neither do I. I have literally fought for my life.
TOM. Really?
LEAH. Yes.

CAL. Like *really* …
LEAH. Yes.
TOM. What happened?
LEAH. Whatever, let's just —
CAL. No come on. You say you could shove a bayonet, you say you've fought for your life. Prove it.
LEAH. Prove it? / Go fuck yourself.
TOM. Leah you don't have to tell us.
CAL. You've heard our shit. / I wanna hear yours.
LEAH. No it's fine, I can tell it — it was a year ago —
A guy attacked me on the subway.
CAL. Someone attacked you?
LEAH. Yeah. I was riding home from a late-night catering job, just a money thing I was doing, and he was the only other person on the train with me. *(She sets up how the subway battle went, mirroring the set up for Pickett's Charge.)*
He was sitting across from me,
like I was here and he was about where that chair is —
and at some point he came over to where I was sitting, pretending to look at the map, like here, and he said, "Excuse me do you know which stop is next?"
And I said "145th" —
and the next thing I knew he was shoving himself on me, like grabbing all over me —
and I couldn't breathe, I'm not sure if he had his hands on my throat, or —
And at first I was sort of paralyzed, like I wasn't sure if he fell over cuz the train jerked or something,
but then when I couldn't breathe and I felt him, like squeezing my breast REALLY hard,
there was this moment that I *understood*
I was being attacked.
And I started screaming — or honestly, it was more like roaring, like a PIG LION or something;
I fucking kicked and screamed with all my might.
And I think I surprised him because he immediately backed off,
or maybe I actually kicked him off —
and he ran to the other end of the train, like to here —
And right then the doors opened and he ran out and that was it.
(Beat.)

TOM. Wow.
CAL. … Okay — I'm sorry — but like, I don't get it. Maybe I don't understand — Some guy grabbed your boob on the subway, right? — Okay sure, yes, that's a bummer, but like — it doesn't sound like — ANTEITAM, you know what I'm saying? / I'm sorry it doesn't.
TOM. (Jesus Christ you are unfuckingbelievable.)
CAL. Oh Tom spare me. You don't fucking get it either, at least / I'm being HONEST.
TOM. I don't get it?
CAL. No you don't
TOM. Okay maybe I don't, maybe I don't get it because I'm a heterosexual male / but at least I know better than to fucking SAY IT.
CAL. Exactly, you're / a fucking faker.
TOM. (Oh mazel tov you get a Courage Cookie for ADMITTING / you're a TOOLBAG.)
CAL. *Mazel tov?!* What the fuck is that?)
TOM. Just shut up Cal.
LEAH. You know what? Fair enough, YES the attack itself was not a fucking WAR, YES there was a major fucking CONTEXT, and YES it had everything to do with being a WOMAN — I don't know if you can possibly understand this, but — The struggle to be a free person — free to do your WORK regardless of your AGE, free to make as much money, free to NOT have a baby, free to be INCLUDED in the shit men get to do — DOES feel like a war — and the thing that makes you — your softness, your — womanness — is your biggest weakness — it's — it's —
CAL. Okay so walk me through this — / I'm serious — *(Cal gets up and gets in Leah's personal space.)*
LEAH. *(Physically uncomfortable.)* (Oh fuck off)
CAL. *(Still advancing.)* A DUDE comes up to you and gets all grabby-grabby — and you kicked him off — that takes balls (excuse the reference) — / absolutely —
LEAH. Get off — !   TOM. Cal —
CAL. So you got him off —
LEAH. GET OFF ME! GET OFF! / GET AWAY FROM ME! JUST GET OFF! GET OFF! GET OFF!
POLITICALLY, METAPHORICALLY, and certainly LITERALLY.

CAL. *(Totally caught off-guard.)* Jesus Christ! Whoah whoah whoah
Jesus Christ! / You KISSED   TOM. Leah?
ME earlier!
LEAH. JUST GET OFF ME! GET. OFF.
(Suddenly — 1863 — fists clenched.)
I am SO SICK
of the STENCH!
I am so sick
of the RUIN
The fighting is done and there are so many bodies.
We cannot carry them,
We cannot bury them
They outnumber us three to one.
We drag them into piles
and as I stop to catch my breath
I am met by their shiny eyelids
their swollen cheeks.
Did I kiss you soldier?
Or you? Or you?
Did I kiss you?
I tell myself that in time
they will dissolve.
The earth will open her mouth, her lips of grass,
And drain it all down
below the streams and the rock
and we will be tempted to forget
those eyelids
those cheeks
But still
they will be there.
*(Leah returns to the present. After a beat — In shock, grappling with
what just happened.)*
Fuck me.
What am I doing??! What — ?!?
CAL. *(Totally lost.)* What just happened? I don't understand —
what …
TOM. Cal. You can't just charge. Do you see that? *(Long beat.)*
CAL. *(Painful realization.)* Am I a dick? Am I just…? *(Beat.)*
LEAH. When I was lining up for the charge today
I heard someone say,

The South is still fighting this war.
And I thought,
Still fighting…?
At what point do you say you lost?
Still fighting means you can't say you lost.
And if you can't say you lost, you can't recover.
I don't want that.
I don't want to look back and realize
I wasn't recovering, I was fighting. *(A beat. Then —)*
CAL. *(About himself.)* But what if you can't…?
You're trying to be a team —
A Union —
and then half wants to quit…?
How do you recover from that?
How does the Mason-Dixon Line not GLOW in the DARK from
all that anguish…? *(Beat.)*
TOM. Maybe you don't.
Maybe you don't recover.
CAL. And then what? *(Beat.)*
TOM. You keep going
But you're still …
LEAH. … Divided. *(A painful beat.)*
TOM. *(Desperate.)* I feel sick.
CAL. Are you okay?
TOM. My stomach is like, in knots.
CAL. Okay.
TOM. I just wanna — eat a popsicle or something.
You know what I mean?
CAL. — ?
No.
TOM. I wanna just — Go home —
and have dreams —
and get up and do my job — and love my wife — and have a baby —
and be okay.
I just wanna be okay.
CAL. You *are* gonna be okay.
TOM. You know what Cal? You say that but you honestly don't
know what you're talking about.
CAL. Tom, what about me? You think you're gonna wanna hang
out and play soldier when your kid's got a soccer game? Fuck no.

Whether you sign or strike you've still got Carrie and a kid comin'
and you're gonna be fine.
TOM. You don't know shit, Cal.
CAL. (Jesus man just / gimme a break)
TOM. I'm serious
CAL. *(Losing patience.)* Look Tom If you're having trouble manning
up or whatever then sign the fucking paper and OWN THAT, don't
take it out on everyone else, Jesus now I get why you play the fuckin'
Deserter every year it's like your sick fantasy or something and now
you're living it out so just do it, go ahead and be a fuckin' coward.
TOM. I'm a coward?   CAL.
                                 Yes

I'M A COWARD

                        YES YOU ARE
(Tom suddenly punches Cal right in the face.)
LEAH. Holy shit
TOM. *(Standing over Cal.)* LOOK AT ME I CAN FIGHT! NOW
AM I BRAVE?? HUH CAL!? NOW AM I BRAVE??!!
CAL. *(Shocked, hurt beyond belief.)* Jesus
TOM. I have known you for over twenty fucking years and you have
not taken a single risk your entire fucking life. Your fiancée bailed.
You don't have a fucking HUMAN BABY coming to permanently
sit at the table of your LIFE. You say faith in the cause, charge for
your cause BUT YOU DON'T HAVE A FUCKING CAUSE
CAL SO WHO IS THE COWARD, HUH? WHO IS THE
FUCKING COWARD?
I mean WHO ARE WE?

…

Who are we?
Who are we?
CAL. *(Gently, desperate.)* Come on dude — enough now
TOM. No really, Cal.
Who are we?
CAL. You're Tom. I'm Cal.
TOM. Who's Tom? Who's Cal?
Why can't we just LOOK DOWN
and see what color we're wearing —
Or LOOK IN FRONT OF US
And SEE a fucking FLAG —
and then we would know which direction to march.

What to kill.
What to save.
But there is no army,
there is no flag
I look down and there's no goddamn uniform.
There's just my shirt.
From the Gap.
That my mother-in-law got me for Christmas.
And it's got FIVE colors in it.
Not one.
Five.
And they're in some dumbass plaid pattern that screams
"HAS NO IDEA WHO HE IS — SHOOT AT WILL."
BANG! BANG! / BANG! BANG!
(Cal tries to hold Tom. Tom pulls away.)
CAL. Tom. Tom.
TOM!
TOM!
TOM. What?! *(Cal takes Tom's face and pulls it close to his.)*
CAL. You're on MY team. Okay?
I'm fucking serious.
I know I'm a dumb asshole but I need you.
You're my cause. You gotta be on my team.
When I look beside me, there's YOU.
TOM. Cal.
CAL. There's you.
TOM. No.
CAL. What do you — ? — don't say that. Yes.
TOM. No, Cal, NO.
When you look beside you, I'm there, but I'm not on your team.
I'm just a GUY.
Fighting his own battle. *(A huge chasm between them. A long beat.)*
I gotta go.
I gotta go home, talk to Carrie …
CAL. Tom —
TOM. *(Not mean.)* Cal, I'm sorry I just — I need to go. *(Cal relents.)*
Leah, I hope I'll see you around town.
LEAH. Well, you know where to find me. Especially if you need
an ugly fabric with American flags on it or whatever.

CAL. *(Who wasn't a part of their earlier conversation.)* Jo-Ann Fabrics
on Route 30?
LEAH. Yes. That's right.
TOM. Okay guys. Good night.
CAL. *(Earnest, desperate to give him something.)* Tom —
Good luck tomorrow.
(Tom nods, starts to exit, then stops. He becomes the Union deserter, 1863.)
DESERTER/TOM. Maybe I'm a piece of shit.
Maybe for the rest of my life
I am a piece of shit.
But even if I were to find a gun, get back in the line,
I'd just be someone else's piece of shit.
At least for the rest of my life
I'm my own piece of shit.
I'm my own. *(With great longing, conjuring the comfort.)*
I'm gonna see my momma.
Eat so much lingonberry pie I feel sick.
Lie in the sun with someone pretty.
Swim the creek
catch crawdads.
I'm gonna sleep on cotton so clean it's a little cool,
smell the magnolia tree —
have good dreams.
I'm gonna see my pappy
Sitting at the table with a Bible,
even though it makes him sore.
Maybe —
the whole goddamn war
will smoke itself out.
We can just — live.
And we can have our pie.
Our pappy.
Our pretty.
We can have our dreams. *(Tom exits.)*
CAL. *(Sadness.)* I love that man. *(Silence. Cal feels his bruised jaw.)*
LEAH. Are you alright?
CAL. I don't know. I guess I should go home.
LEAH. *(Gently.)* Yeah, me too. I work tomorrow. *(They stand, start
to leave.)*
CAL. *(Stops.)* (Aw fuck.) Hey Leah.

LEAH. Hey yeah.

CAL. I know that like, I've firmly established myself as a meathead douchebag of like, mythic proportion …

LEAH. Yes.

CAL. And I know — it's really awkward right now and timing is really shitty — and I don't even know if you'd even want to hang out with me after this… But there's a dance next week — it's basically a barn dance to raise money to preserve Civil War barns in Adams County — and I was wondering if you'd like to go …

LEAH. Cal — that's — / um —

CAL. I mean, it'll be in FULL REGALIA. Just to warn you.

LEAH. Full Regalia

CAL. Yeah, like the white gloves and everything.

LEAH. Okay.

CAL. I mean, I don't know if you happen to know any of the dances of the era, but like,

I could teach you a few … There'll be a full period band, the whole nine. Tom will be there — Or — well — I don't know I hope Tom will be there … *(Beat.)* So what do you think?

LEAH. I don't know Cal. My Farby point status is still pretty bad.

CAL. Yeah, that's a good point. *(He thinks for a moment. Like, too long of a moment.)*

LEAH. Jesus Christ are you seriously thinking of revoking your invitation (which I have not accepted by the way) because I might not have a fucking HOOP SKIRT??!

CAL. No no. I was thinking MAYBE I could come by Jo-Ann Fabrics tomorrow and we could pick out a fabric and get you a dress made. My mom is actually really good at that shit and she totally loves it, and like, it'll make her year.

LEAH. You're being serious — A dress — like with a hoop and everything.

CAL. Yeah.

LEAH. Is this a plot to get me to stop being a soldier on the battlefield? Like if I have a fucking hoop dress I'll stop re-enacting the battles…?

CAL. No no no. Seriously. I just thought you might like the dance …

LEAH. And —

CAL. *(Sincere.)* And I thought it would be really fun to have you. As my friend.

LEAH. So your mom will make me a hoop dress out of an ugly fabric of my choosing —
CAL. (Which hopefully will be 1863-appropriate)
LEAH. And then you and I will do the fuckin' Schottische, or whatever —
CAL. *(Utterly delighted.)* (Oooh, that's a good one, I'm impressed you know that)
LEAH. And then I can put on my Confederate soldier outfit and drink with the boys afterward if I want to.
CAL. *(Loves it.)* Wowza. Yes.
LEAH. Okay Cal.
CAL. Okay?
LEAH. Yeah. Okay. So I guess I'll see you at Jo-ann Fabrics.
CAL. Yes you will. Tomorrow.
LEAH. Okay. And Cal … I don't know … Maybe Tom will be there. *(He nods. Then with surprising tenderness — he salutes her.)*
CAL. Goodnight Leah. *(She salutes back.)*
LEAH. Goodnight Cal.
(Leah exits. Cal/Longstreet is alone with his anguish. He picks up the Union jacket that Tom left behind. Holds it tenderly for a moment. 1863. The sound of crickets.)
LONGSTREET/CAL. I cannot sleep.
The day's charge is done,
and even now I hear the dead.
Their arms outstretched, their terrible cry
As they hurl to a darkness where I cannot help.
The night is thick with moth dust, and hot,
So I walk out among the tents, like ghostly triangles,
Where what's left of my men,
Row after row,
lie dreaming in the dark.
Long dreams, like rope,
pulling them toward tomorrow's long march back.
And for one quiet moment,
it's just a pretty summer night …
(He looks right at the audience. Truly takes them in.)
When suddenly
I see them there —
sitting right up, looking right at me —
The Future

Solemn and serene
they are looking at me.
While my men sleep,
their future selves are alert, like deer.
They look at me expectantly, like they await my command.
Or do I await theirs?
I know not.
But here we stand — eye to eye —
The Future
And me.
(Still with the audience — quietly, with deep yearning.)
Will we do it?
Will we form
A More Perfect Union?
We must, right?
Surely we must …
But I look into their bright, flickering eyes
and I only see
the outline of my gray coat, my tired hair.
I only see the obscured darkness of my own face.
Do they know
That below them sleep and dream — themselves?
Do they know
Of the terrible cost?
What can I offer you
But my desperate
Blind
Resolve?
What can I do for you
But charge?
(After a moment.)
I raise my hand —
*(He raises his hand to the audience, solemnly, like he's taking an oath,
or about to wave.)*
White in the dark,
like coral, or a flag —
And with my hand raised to the Future —
I say
Hello.
Hold.

Help.
I say
I promise.
I say
Peace.
I say
Goodnight.

End of Play

PROPERTY LIST

Civil War-era gun with bayonet
Haversack
Canteen
Gun powder
Beer glasses
Paper napkin

SOUND EFFECTS

Close battle (marching, cannons, guns, etc.)
Marching
Battle at a distance
Cannon fire
Bird chirping

NEW PLAYS

★ **BENGAL TIGER AT THE BAGHDAD ZOO by Rajiv Joseph.** The lives of two American Marines and an Iraqi translator are forever changed by an encounter with a quick-witted tiger who haunts the streets of war-torn Baghdad. "[A] boldly imagined, harrowing and surprisingly funny drama." *–NY Times.* "Tragic yet darkly comic and highly imaginative." *–CurtainUp.* [5M, 2W] ISBN: 978-0-8222-2565-2

★ **THE PITMEN PAINTERS by Lee Hall, inspired by a book by William Feaver.** Based on the triumphant true story, a group of British miners discover a new way to express themselves and unexpectedly become art-world sensations. "Excitingly ambiguous, in-the-moment theater." *–NY Times.* "Heartfelt, moving and deeply politicized." *–Chicago Tribune.* [5M, 2W] ISBN: 978-0-8222-2507-2

★ **RELATIVELY SPEAKING by Ethan Coen, Elaine May and Woody Allen.** In TALKING CURE, Ethan Coen uncovers the sort of insanity that can only come from family. Elaine May explores the hilarity of passing in GEORGE IS DEAD. In HONEYMOON MOTEL, Woody Allen invites you to the sort of wedding day you won't forget. "Firecracker funny." *–NY Times.* "A rollicking good time." *–New Yorker.* [8M, 7W] ISBN: 978-0-8222-2394-8

★ **SONS OF THE PROPHET by Stephen Karam.** If to live is to suffer, then Joseph Douaihy is more alive than most. With unexplained chronic pain and the fate of his reeling family on his shoulders, Joseph's health, sanity, and insurance premium are on the line. "Explosively funny." *–NY Times.* "At once deep, deft and beautifully made." *–New Yorker.* [5M, 3W] ISBN: 978-0-8222-2597-3

★ **THE MOUNTAINTOP by Katori Hall.** A gripping reimagination of events the night before the assassination of the civil rights leader Dr. Martin Luther King, Jr. "An ominous electricity crackles through the opening moments." *–NY Times.* "[A] thrilling, wild, provocative flight of magical realism." *–Associated Press.* "Crackles with theatricality and a humanity more moving than sainthood." *–NY Newsday.* [1M, 1W] ISBN: 978-0-8222-2603-1

★ **ALL NEW PEOPLE by Zach Braff.** Charlie is 35, heartbroken, and just wants some time away from the rest of the world. Long Beach Island seems to be the perfect escape until his solitude is interrupted by a motley parade of misfits who show up and change his plans. "Consistently and sometimes sensationally funny." *–NY Times.* "A morbidly funny play about the trendy new existential condition of being young, adorable, and miserable." *–Variety.* [2M, 2W] ISBN: 978-0-8222-2562-1

DRAMATISTS PLAY SERVICE, INC.
440 Park Avenue South, New York, NY 10016 212-683-8960 Fax 212-213-1539
postmaster@dramatists.com www.dramatists.com

NEW PLAINS

★ **CLYBOURNE PARK by Bruce Norris.** WINNER OF THE 2011 PULITZER PRIZE AND 2012 TONY AWARD. Act One takes place in 1959 as community leaders try to stop the sale of a home to a black family. Act Two is set in the same house in the present day as the now predominantly African-American neighborhood battles to hold its ground. "Vital, sharp-witted and ferociously smart." *–NY Times.* "A theatrical treasure…Indisputably, uproariously funny." *–Entertainment Weekly.* [4M, 3W] ISBN: 978-0-8222-2697-0

★ **WATER BY THE SPOONFUL by Quiara Alegría Hudes.** WINNER OF THE 2012 PULITZER PRIZE. A Puerto Rican veteran is surrounded by the North Philadelphia demons he tried to escape in the service. "This is a very funny, warm, and yes uplifting play." *–Hartford Courant.* "The play is a combination poem, prayer and app on how to cope in an age of uncertainty, speed and chaos." *–Variety.* [4M, 3W] ISBN: 978-0-8222-2716-8

★ **RED by John Logan.** WINNER OF THE 2010 TONY AWARD. Mark Rothko has just landed the biggest commission in the history of modern art. But when his young assistant, Ken, gains the confidence to challenge him, Rothko faces the agonizing possibility that his crowning achievement could also become his undoing. "Intense and exciting." *–NY Times.* "Smart, eloquent entertainment." *–New Yorker.* [2M] ISBN: 978-0-8222-2483-9

★ **VENUS IN FUR by David Ives.** Thomas, a beleaguered playwright/director, is desperate to find an actress to play Vanda, the female lead in his adaptation of the classic sadomasochistic tale *Venus in Fur.* "Ninety minutes of good, kinky fun." *–NY Times.* "A fast-paced journey into one man's entrapment by a clever, vengeful female." *–Associated Press.* [1M, 1W] ISBN: 978-0-8222-2603-1

★ **OTHER DESERT CITIES by Jon Robin Baitz.** Brooke returns home to Palm Springs after a six-year absence and announces that she is about to publish a memoir dredging up a pivotal and tragic event in the family's history—a wound they don't want reopened. "Leaves you feeling both moved and gratifyingly sated." *–NY Times.* "A genuine pleasure." *–NY Post.* [2M, 3W] ISBN: 978-0-8222-2605-5

★ **TRIBES by Nina Raine.** Billy was born deaf into a hearing family and adapts brilliantly to his family's unconventional ways, but it's not until he meets Sylvia, a young woman on the brink of deafness, that he finally understands what it means to be understood. "A smart, lively play." *–NY Times.* "[A] bright and boldly provocative drama." *–Associated Press.* [3M, 2W] ISBN: 978-0-8222-2751-9

DRAMATISTS PLAY SERVICE, INC.
440 Park Avenue South, New York, NY 10016 212-683-8960 Fax 212-213-1539
postmaster@dramatists.com www.dramatists.com